"Eat The Way
YOU
Want to Look"
Cookbook

A follow up cookbook to the bestseller

"The Edible Fountain of Youth" ™

Author
Susan M. Poore

RN, CNC, CPLC, CHP ~ Healthy Aging Expert

www.TheEdibleFountainOfYouth.com

First Edition 2016

Professional Photos by Melissa Stokes @ Mack Visuals

Cover Design by Rob Williams

Edited by Gerri Shepherd

I dedicate this book to ...

All of my friends, family, patients, attendees of my cooking classes and for those who have enjoyed many of my recipes over the years.

A special thanks to all of you for encouraging me to pack a few dozen healthy recipes into this cookbook to share with the world.

"Eat The Way YOU Want to Look" ™

The Edible Fountain of Youth
EAT THE WAY YOU WANT TO LOOK

Contents

As you will notice, many of my recipes are named after my family members – my parents, children, grandchildren, siblings, husband, nieces, nephews and my sweet cat.

They are my recipes - simply with their names added to them! I did it to add some fun and create memories for them about my cookbook. Life is good!

Good Nutrition in Every Meal...

"Wrap"-ing it up with Sandwiches and Pita's!

Cold Fresh Salads Are More Than Iceberg Lettuce!

Love a GREAT Soup or Chili...

Those Darn Healthy Desserts!

Snacks ...Toppings... And More!

In 2016, my company is launching a new product:

"The Edible Fountain of Youth Smoothie Packet"

It's perfect for "Heathy Aging Nuts" and will contain all the *key ingredients* you need to keep inflammation intact and your immune system at its peak performance.

Watch for its release date on our website:

www.TheEdibleFountainOfYouth.com

We will also announce it on social media and advertise it around the country. I appreciate everyone who is excited for us and we look forward to sharing this product with others!

An opening note to my readers...

"We Are What We Eat"

Powerful words. Most people believe those words but do not want to put in the effort that it takes to "Eat the Way YOU Want to Look.". We all know that eating healthy is what gives us the best chance for a long life without the multitudes of diseases that face our population, especially as we age.

We also know that with the right healthy eating plan, our skin improves, our energy improves and every cell in our body responds in a positive way. The opposite can happen with the SAD diet - Standard American Diet.

There comes a time in your life when you look in the mirror and decide – THIS IS IT. Let's reflect on a few thoughts...

Over the years you may have said to yourself →

- "I will start tomorrow", you know the infamous manana syndrome.
- "I will eat it only one more time"
- "It can't be that bad for me"
- "Eating healthy is hard"
- "I love ALL the foods that I know are bad for me"
- "I hate my body, my fat roles and my cholesterol"

Let me ask you a couple of direct questions. Do you want to look like a "processed food?" Not really understanding what's inside you? Not really knowing what you are made of and how your health is? Of course not.

Or would you rather be healthy and vibrant, like "real plant foods" are? Want to have color, energy and a positive glow about you? Want to feel and look great, where nothing can stop you? I vote for healthy and vibrant!

In my book "The Edible Fountain of Youth", I share stories of real patients with real struggles. In my years in practice, I have seen first handed what a poor diet can do and then in amazement what a healthy plant based diet can do.

This cookbook was written with all types of people in mind. **You will not see any meat recipes in here.** Primarily because the majority of people know how to cook meat. Their struggles are with the vegetables, grains, etc. that accompany the meat. If you aren't on a plant based diet, I hope to inspire you to eat more plant based meals and make the meat your "side dish" instead of the other way around. *If you are vegan – there may be just a few ingredients you need to avoid and/or substitute.* These recipes are written for the average person who wants to learn how to make plant based dishes taste well and not take all day to create.

Like all my books, I write the way I speak, with kindness, honesty and hope to give you the information you need to live a blessed and healthy life - through good nutrition. It's no different for this cookbook.

This book is simple and straight forward. You don't need hundreds of recipes to narrow down a few great ones. Understand, that recipes do not need to be difficult or have so many ingredients that it's a real task to put it together. *I am very much like you, I just want to create a dish that is delicious along with being a very healthy meal.*

"There is no diet out there

that will do what healthy eating does"

Skip the diet. Just eat healthy.

Healthy Tips & Suggestions

- Even though each ingredient in my cookbook may not have "organic" written in front of it, they all should be. I personally use between 80-100% "organic" ingredients in my creations. The only time I may not, is if it is not available in my small town or online. Love organic shopping! *Why you ask?* We are already exposed to way too many chemicals in our environment and also when we travel and dine. So if I can give my body the best of the best while home, I am going to do just that!

- Plant based – what exactly does that mean? In America, our current state of mind is to include an animal protein with every meal. Many profound and very reputable studies have shown that the increase in animal products and processed foods along with the decrease in whole plant based foods over the past 50 years is killing our country. *The shift to a plant based diet could save BILLIONS of dollars in health care cost alone.* Plant based means that you are centering your diet around plants, legumes, nuts and seeds. What we eat greatly influences our personal health and the global environment. I follow a plant based diet closely for my health. Read "The China Study" to better understand the effect on your health and longevity when you move to a plant based diet.

- Cooking with Flax Eggs. Unless you create a recipe where your boiling the egg and/or placing it on top (i.e. salad) or actually eating it (i.e. fried, poached, etc.), you really don't need eggs to bake. If you're looking for a fluffier baked good, then you may consider an egg. I personally do not consume eggs. Flaxseed can have a huge impact on your health, both in terms of nutrition and the quality of the baked good. If lowering your cholesterol and adding more heart healthy omega-3 fatty acids is your goal, use ground flaxseeds in place of eggs.

- Salt – even though I list it on some of the recipes, I highly suggest only using salt "to taste." So many other herbs can create great results without causing some of the issues that too much salt can do. When I do use salt, I use Himalayan Pink Sea Salt or a Hawaiian Black Sea Salt because both are both nutrient dense compared to table salt.

- Applesauce replacement for oil in baking. I love to substitute applesauce because it cuts down on the fat and calories. I use an "Organic Unsweetened Applesauce" and keep a small 6 pack of individual cups in my pantry for convenience. FYI: The sweetened varieties add extra sugar and they can also alter the texture of the baked goods. The cinnamon flavor or other flavorings will change the taste. So I stick with the plain unsweetened and add extra spices if needed. FYI: I measure applesauce in a glass measuring cup. Whatever the recipe calls for it, I use ¾ the amount. For example, say the recipe calls for 1 cup of oil, use ¾ cup of applesauce. Then if the batter seems dry, you can add 1-2 tbsp. more to consistency!

- How to ripen an avocado overnight: Put an avocado in a brown paper bag with a couple of apples, set on the counter. In the am your avocado will have softened. The avocado is a superfood that is eaten quite frequently in our household.

- Chia seeds: What do I love about these power house seeds? (1) They deliver a massive amount of nutrients with a small amount of calories. (2) They are high in Omega-3 fatty acids, protein and essential amino acids. (3) Almost all the carbs in them are fiber. (4) Great for weight loss and your gastrointestinal system. (6) Chia seeds are high in nutrients that important for bone health. This includes calcium, phosphorus, magnesium and protein. (7) Easy to incorporate into your diet and a healthy aging eating plan. (8) They are literally loaded with antioxidants.

- Greens, the LEADER of all superfoods. Add greens in your diet every chance you get. Green veggies, herbs and spices have more of an impact on our health than any other food on this blessed earth!

- Herbs, Spices and Essential Oils. Wow, all three can take a boring meal and turn it into a wonderful full flavor dish to enjoy. Using herbs and spices can help decrease the inflammatory process that occurs in our bodies. I recently learned a tremendous amount about essential oils, what they can do for our brain, health and body. I have learned how they will impact my healthy aging programs. My goal is to incorporate them into my recipes more often (another book in my future?)

- Grains, Seeds and Legumes. Don't be afraid to experiment with any of these. Many people consume their "routine" daily foods day in and day out - never learning to try different foods that may drastically improve their health. Don't do this...

Bottom line...

The MORE superfoods you can add into your
diet on a daily basis, the better!

Read more about the power of superfoods in my book,

"The Edible Fountain of Youth"

Healthy Aging ROCKS!

Starting Your Morning With a RUSH of NUTRIENTS...

Jean's Just After Sunrise Power Breakfast

There is nothing better than a nice warm healthy breakfast. For many of us, it brings back childhood memories. I love taking oatmeal and adding a variety of tastes, textures and superfoods to my bowl. Just like many of my recipes, you can change it up, replace as needed or add extra additives that you may enjoy.

Remember, anytime you can add any "green veggie" to your meals, you are "superfood-izing it!"

This recipe results in about 3 cups.

Gather ingredients:

2 large pretty ripe bananas (they are sweeter)

2 medium carrots (lightly packed to 3/4th cup after grating)

½ cup zucchini

2 tablespoons chia seeds

1 cup rolled oats (can use gluten free if needed)

2 ¼ cups nut milk (I use unsweented vanilla almond milk)

1 – 1 ½ teaspoons cinnamon, to taste

2 Tbsp. hemp hearts

Dash of sea salt (optional)

Create it...

In a medium bowl, mash the banana until almost smooth. The softer the banana the better because it provides a natural sweetener to this delicious morning meal. Place it into a medium pot.

Using fine hole grater, grate the carrots and measure till you have about 3/4th of a cup lightly packed. When done add it to the pot with the banana. Using the same grater, grate the zucchini then place it into the pot too.

Add the rolled oats, nut milk and chia seeds into the pot. Stir well.

Heat in uncovered pot on medium to cook the oats, stir frequently and decrease heat if necessary. Cook about 10-15 minutes until the oats are soft and the mixture is thick. When done cooking add the hemp seeds (great protein) and the cinnamon to taste.

If desired, you can sprinkle walnut bits on top before serving. If the mixture is too thin, add a little flax, if too thick, add a little nut milk to thin out to a good consistency.

If you have any leftovers, you can store them in an airtight container in your refrigerator for an additional day making breakfast ready to go tomorrow.

Powerful breakfast that your body and mind will benefit from!

Summer's Pumpkin Spiced Pancakes

Pumpkin flavored anything is great in our household. Pumpkin is nutrient dense and has a remarkable amount of vitamins and antioxidants in it. I believe you will love this recipe. I got it online quite a while ago and have changed it around a bit. Delicious.

Gather ingredients:

¾ cup unsweetened vanilla almond milk*

1 Tbsp. lemon juice

1/3 cup organic packed pumpkin puree (not the pre-mix)

1 Tbsp. butter (I use Earth Balance for Vegans or melted coconut oil.

½ tsp pure vanilla extract

3 Tbsp. organic brown sugar

1 Tbsp. REAL maple syrup

1 tsp. baking powder

½ tsp baking soda

Just a pinch salt

1 tsp. pumpkin pie spice

¼ tsp cinnamon

1 cup whole wheat pastry flour

Create it...

Pre-heat skillet to medium-low heat. The surface should be hot but not scalding hot. The coconut oil you use should not burn when it hits the surface.

Combine ¾ cup milk and lemon juice in a large bowl and let rest for 5 minutes to curdle. Add the melted butter, maple syrup, pumpkin, brown sugar, vanilla extract and whisk them all together.

Next add flour, baking soda, baking powder, salt and spices to a sifter. Sift together over the wet ingredients. If the batter appears too thin, add a bit more flour. If too thick, add a splash of almond milk. If too thin, add a bit more flour. Let batter rest for 5-10 minutes.

Spray your pan then pour ¼ cups of the batter onto the skillet. It will make 5-6 pancakes depending on how large you make them. Flip over when bubbles appear in the middle and the edges turn slightly dry. Cook for 1-3 minutes more on the other side, then flip onto your plate.

Top with real maple syrup and if you desire, a dash of pumpkin pie spice or cinnamon.

*Start with ¾ cup of almond milk. If the batter is too thick after mixing, add the remaining amount in Tbsp. increments. Thickness will depend on your pumpkin puree and whether you used maple syrup or honey or agave.

Brew a cup of tea or coffee to enjoy these pancakes with!

Kinley's (Keen-Wa) Quinoa Blueberry Pancakes

Blueberries are one of the superfoods that can improve your health especially when you routinely consume them. I eat blueberries every morning in my smoothie. My mother, Jean, has a serious addiction to this super fruit. So when I think of this recipe, I think of her. Mix it with the quinoa grain and you have a super healthy breakfast!

Gather ingredients:

1 ½ cups all-purpose flour OR use a gluten free flour (with xanthan gum – a plant based thickener)

½ cup quinoa flour

2 teaspoons baking powder

1 teaspoon sea salt (or less)

⅓ cup coconut palm sugar

3 flax mixed eggs

¼ cup unsweetened applesauce

1 ½ cups of nut milk (I prefer unsweetened almond)

1 teaspoon vanilla extract

4 tablespoons melted Earth Balance – Organic Vegan

1 ½ cups cooked quinoa

1 cup fresh blueberries (if using frozen, defrost and drain)

Create it...

In a medium bowl combine flours, baking powder, sea salt and coconut palm sugar.

Prepare flax eggs → Takes one tbsp. of GROUND flax and 3 tbsp. of water to replace ONE egg – so triple it for this recipe. Mix together in small bowl, stir well, let sit for 10-15 minutes, then ready. Then add to the applesauce, milk, vanilla and butter. Whisk in the dry ingredients.

In a separate bowl add flax eggs to the batter and mix well. Stir in quinoa.

Preheat a griddle or nonstick pan to med/high. Lightly oil. Drop the batter onto the warm pan. When the batter begins to set, add in blueberries. They can be served by themselves or with real maple syrup drizzled lightly for flavor.

Blueberries and quinoa will rock the start of your day!

☺ ☺ ☺

Breakfast Muffins with Carrots & Zucchini

Veggies, fruits, no added sugar. Have loved these muffins for a long time. Great with green tea or a cup of java for breakfast. Also makes a tasty midafternoon snack. Kids love them too and they are super healthy!

Heat oven to 350°F.

Gather ingredients...

¼ cup pitted prunes

½ cup dates

1 ¼ cups whole wheat pastry flour

¼ Tsp. baking soda

2 Tsp. baking powder

2 Tsp. ground cinnamon

Pinch of nutmeg

½ Tsp. sea salt

2 ripe mashed bananas

¼ cup nut milk (I used unsweetened vanilla almond milk)

½ cup shredded zucchini, squeeze out any moisture

2 shredded carrots

½ cup unsweetened applesauce

½ cup golden raisins

Create it...

Soak the prunes and dates in warm water for 10-12 minutes. Then drain a couple of times till they are smooth/dry.

In the meantime, mix all the dry ingredients (spices, flour, baking powder and baking soda) together in a bowl, then set aside.

Take a medium mixing bowl, combine dates, prunes, bananas, zucchini, carrots, applesauce, and nut milk. Mix until smooth then add dry ingredients slowly mixing as you go. Do NOT over mix. When done add raisins and mix to combine.

Line your muffin tins, grease or simply spray it with a nonstick spray. Fill each muffin tin ¾ full.

Bake for 30 minutes @ 350 degrees. You will know when ready when your toothpick comes out clean. Remove from oven and let cool. Transfer to a wire cooling rack.

Muffins will stay fresh if placed in an airtight container at room temperature for up to 4 days. If your house is like mine, they won't last that long!

Brew some green tea or coffee and enjoy...

Patsy's Pepitas & Banana Salad

Those of us that enjoy bananas and pepitas will love this combo. Pepitas (pumpkin seeds) are powerful and contain a wide variety of nutrients (protein, magnesium, manganese, copper and zinc.) They also contain phytosterols along with antioxidants. Mix them with a super spice – cinnamon and fruit and you have a healthy breakfast or snack treat!

This serves 2, but I double the recipe because it is so good!

Gather ingredients:

1 large RIPE but not real brown banana (makes the dish sweeter)

1 large ripe pear (I use the Asian variety; it tastes great)

½ fresh lime

½ tsp. organic Vietnamese Saigon Cinnamon (it has a superior flavor)

2 oz. "toasted" Pepitas (toast in the oven)

Create it...

Prepare the fruit. Clean. Peel the banana and slice into ¼ inch rounds. Peel the pear and dice into ¾ inch pieces. Squeeze the fresh lime over the cut fruit and let that sit for 10 minutes.

Top the salad with the toasted Pepitas.

If you'd like, you can add additional fresh herbs or sprinkle ground flax seed on the top.

This is a simple salad with a lot of flavor that your breakfast guest will love...

Life is so SMOOTHIE!

Smoothies have become quite a trend and I hope they are here to stay. I was NOT always a big fan. I thought that drinking my calories could quickly add up and I would rather enjoy every morsel of food. I saw so many people fill their smoothies with high caloric/high sugar ingredients that could cause more inflammation in their bodies or weight on their frames. Sugary thick drinks, I knew, was not what I needed to keep me healthy.

Then one day I was watching David Wolfe (a VERY well respected health expert) advertise for the NutriBullet. I have respected David for years. His knowledge in the nutrition and health conscious world is very impressive. So I decided to research the device and seek healthy recipes that I could share with my patients and audiences at seminars.

I purchased a Nutri Bullet and the rest is history. What I found after only 2 weeks of daily raw drinks was an energy I had never felt before. It wasn't that I was blending my foods, it was that I was putting in several key ingredients and ONLY health promoting, not inflammatory foods. This part is very important.

I know that if I am traveling (which I do often with my business) then I have to be sure I start the day out right. Traveling diets are not the best. I wanted to show how it could be done. I travel with my pre-made containers of additives and stop at grocery stores for the fresh stuff along the way. My NutriBullet has literally traveled with me for thousands of miles and hundreds of trips. If I can do it – so can you.

My daily raw green drink has over 21+ ingredients in it and literally covers what we all really need in our diets for exceptional longevity. It has improved my health drastically.

Super healthy smoothies can benefit many, especially...

- Those who do not consume enough veggies and fruits throughout the day.
- Those who know that they do not eat well and need denser nutrients included into their diets.
- Those whose immune systems are at risk or during "cold & flu" seasons.

- Those who want a simple, quick and healthy start to their day.
- Those who really want to live the healthy aging lifestyle and feed their cells high nutrients daily.
- People who want exceptional health, period!

When I first started making the smoothies, I had all these different containers or bags the ingredients were purchased in. It was a hassle to open each container every day and quite frankly if it becomes hard, most people will give it up after a very short time.

So I decided to minimize my frustration and make it work well. So I purchased large glass containers and put all the dry ingredients in them. If you do this, be sure your containers seal well. Many of the ingredients can get bad fast if left out to air or if not sealed well.

I then bought small containers (24 of them) and once every 24 days I line them up on my counter and fill them from the jars. I use the non-BPA disposable containers. You can use them dozens of times over and over because everything you put in there is dry. This has made a HUGE difference. I actually started out with just 12 containers but found that 12 days seem to go by really fast, 24 seems to work for me....30 may be better for you.

☺ ☺ ☺

Karsyn's Kool Kranberry Kale Kooler

Kale is a MAJOR superfood! I love this recipe because it starts out with a "green" that most people don't want to eat raw or even consider buying because they don't know what to do with it. I use kale in a variety of ways. Adding it to soups and stir-fry's is super easy. But now that I have been adding it to smoothies, I get my Vitamin K in every day. Anti-aging rock star!

Around the holidays, you are able to purchase fresh cranberries. I throw them into the freezer to use for my smoothies throughout the year. If you can do this too, it will increase the fiber and Vitamin C in your Kool Kooler!

Gather ingredients:

1 cups fresh kale

½ cup fresh cranberries with 1 cup water OR ¾ cups of unsweetened cranberry juice

¼ cup water

1 orange, peeled

1 frozen banana (I buy them when on sale, break in thirds and freeze in a Ziploc bag). Using a frozen fruit makes any smoothie thicker and cold.

¼ of a fresh lime squeezed

Create it...

Put your frozen fruit in 1st if using the bullet, last if using a blender then follow with all of the other ingredients. Keep blending till done. Pour into glass and put a lime wedge on the edge for fun!

Completely kool off with this kranberry kooler!!

☺ ☺ ☺

Poore's Paradise Island Smoothie

This is a great smoothie to enjoy on a warm day while you are sitting on the beach, around your pool or just dreaming of your next vacation! It kind of tastes like a Pina Colada.

Gather ingredients:

1 cup of fresh spinach

1 ½ cups frozen pineapple

½ cup coconut milk

½ cup water

1-2 tablespoons of unsweetened coconut flakes to taste

Create it...

Blend together all of the ingredients.

If you use fresh pineapple, you may need to add some ice to give it more of a slush consistency. Fresh fruit needs a little less water because it's a bit juicer.

Whip this together, put a thin slice of fresh pineapple on the edge and you will be thinking of a Jimmy Buffett song!

☺ ☺ ☺

Susan's Super Skin Smoothie

I came up with this recipe when I wanted to use an avocado in my smoothie. Besides being great for your heart, an avocado has huge skin benefits. Very good for healthy aging from the inside out. We live in the southwest so having this amazing "fruit" (yes it is a fruit) in our refrigerator ready to use is great.

Gather ingredients:

1 cup of frozen pineapple

1 cup of unsweetened coconut water (I keep 1-2 container in my pantry at all times)

1 ½ cups of fresh spinach

1/4 of a ripe avocado

Create it...

Blend all ingredients together, drink it 2-3 times a week.

Watch closely, your skin will thank you!

☺ ☺ ☺

Cy's Chocolate Raspberry

In Heaven Smoothie

Chocolate is well loved by many. The cacao bean (a superfood) is what chocolate is made from. This smoothie is a great anti-inflammatory thick healthy snack for when you want ice cream or chocolate but know that you don't want high calories or fat, but you need your chocolate fix!

Gather ingredients:

½ - ¾ cup of frozen raspberries (to taste)

1 medium banana (fresh or frozen as long as the raspberries are frozen to make it thick/cold)

1 cup milk of almond milk (or another nut milk)

1 tbsp. cacao powder

1 tbsp. of chocolate pea protein powder

1 tbsp. of chia seed gel (see Tip & Suggestions)

Maple syrup or honey *to taste* (could also use an organic Stevia)

½ tbsp. of coconut flakes

¼ tsp. cinnamon

Create it...

Put all ingredients into your blender or bullet.

Then be ready to get your "Chocolate Fix" on!!!

☺ ☺ ☺

Chris' Cilantro Island Smoothie

Great simple smoothie with lots of island flavor!!!

Gather ingredients:

½ cup of <u>EACH</u>

- frozen papaya
- pineapple
- mango chunks

¼ of a ripe avocado

1 cup water

¼ - ½ cup cilantro

½ of a lime

Create it...

Put fruit, avocado and cilantro into a bowl. Squeeze ½ of a lime over ingredient.

Sprinkle a very small amount of Himalayan sea salt and ginger powder into mix to taste. (Mix 1st, taste, then add)

Place into your blender or NutriBullet.

It is a beautiful drink to relax with on a lazy day thinking about nothing but you being on an island...

☺ ☺ ☺

Kellan's Berry Healthy Smoothie

Berries are so nutrient dense that any time you need to pick a fruit, if a berry is available – pick it. Major superfood!

Gather ingredients:

½ cup of frozen blueberries

½ banana

1 tsp ground flaxseed

1 Tbsp. hemp or pea protein powder

Handful of spinach or spring mix

Handful of kale

1 cup of a nut milk (I use unsweetened vanilla almond)

Create it...

Put it all into your blender or bullet. Blend until smooth.

Your heart and immune system will thank you!

Good Nutrition in Every Days Meal...

Black Bean Veggie Enchiladas

This is a delicious and easy dish to put together. It is robust, very filling and packed with protein. Replacing the animal protein with veggies will improve your health without a doubt. I got this recipe online and have changed it up quite a few times to make it my own. Enough for about 4 servings – double it now and make a second pan right away for another meal!

Heat oven to 400 degrees.

Gather ingredients:

2 cups enchilada sauce (homemade or store bought)

2 Tbsp. extra virgin olive oil or coconut oil

1 chopped up red bell pepper

1 cup red onion chopped in small pieces

½ head of broccoli

½ small head of cauliflower florets, slice into thin pieces

1 tsp. cumin

¼ tsp. ground cinnamon

5 cups of packed spinach

1½ cups cooked black beans (if you use canned, use one BPA free15 oz. can, drain and rinse it very well)

1 cup shredded Monterey Jack cheese, divided

Cheese optional. This dish can be made VEGAN. You can skip the cheese altogether and still end up with awesome enchiladas. For creaminess, add soft sliced avocado for some extra creaminess. Or use a vegan cheese that can totally replace it and add a wonderful taste.

Salt and pepper to taste...

Use 8 – 8" whole wheat tortillas   This recipe can be made GLUTEN FREE by using a certified gluten-free "flour" tortillas. If you do use corn tortillas, you may need to use more because of their size and gently warm them before you try to roll them up, or they might break in half.

Create it...

Heat your oven to 400 degrees.

I place my racks with one in the middle of the oven and then the other in the upper third. I lightly grease a 13 x 9-inch pan with coconut oil or cooking spray.

Drizzle a little oil in a large skillet over medium heat, until warm. Throw in the onions, cooking 5-7 min or until the onions are soft and translucent. Next, add the broccoli and bell peppers, cover it and reduce heat to medium-low. Stir occasionally until the broccoli is a brighter green and begins to turn golden on the edges.

Add the cumin and cinnamon to the skillet and stir, let it cook about 30-45 seconds, then add the spinach, a few handfuls at a time cooking until all the spinach has wilted into the pan.

Pour all the pan ingredients into a medium mixing bowl. Add black beans (drained), ¼ cup cheese and 2 tbsp. of enchilada sauce. Season with fresh ground pepper and salt (optional) to taste.

Putting your enchiladas together:

Pour ¼ cup enchilada sauce into your prepared pan - work it around the bottom so it is evenly coated.

Take one tortilla, spread ½ cup filling mixture down the middle of it, make a wrap by bringing the left side over and then the right. Place the seam side down against the edge of your pan. Repeat with all the remaining tortillas and filling.

Drizzle the remaining enchilada sauce evenly over the enchiladas. Leave the tips/the edges of the enchiladas bare. Sprinkle the remaining shredded cheese evenly over the entire dish.

Bake, uncovered, on the middle rack for 20 minutes. If you are using cheese and the top isn't golden enough for you, move the pan to the upper rack and bake for an additional 4 to 6 minutes, until it is golden.

When you remove the pan from the oven, let it rest for at least 10 minutes so they set. I sprinkle chopped cilantro on the top of each then serve immediately.

Mexican food is loved by so many people and this recipe can be flexible as far as the veggies go. You can add a little green chile or different beans if you desire. Serve with a salad and blue organic chips with salsa – *muy bueno... delicioso!*

☺ ☺ ☺

Natasha's Nutritious Quinoa Quiche

This dish has a great flavor and so many health benefits. It's high in fiber, vegan and gluten free, contains lots of protein and calcium. It has no crust and is super easy to prepare!

Heat oven to 375 degrees.

Gather ingredients:

Prepare 3 cups cooked quinoa. I make mine in my rice cooker (best invention ever.) For every 1 cup of quinoa, add 1 ¾ cups of water. So with this recipe, put 3 cups of quinoa into the rice cooker, add 5 ¼ cups of water. Super simple and done in no time at all.

4 flax eggs. If you have never used them, you will be amazed how well they work and you cannot tell the difference but your body will. To make, mix ¼ cup flax meal to ¾ cup of water, mix and then let it sit until thickened, usually takes 5-10 min.

½ cup of a nut milk + 2 Tbsp. (I use unsweetened almond)

1 Tbsp. baking powder

8 cups packed kale with no stems. (8 oz.)

½ cup red minced onion

½ cup minced celery

1½ cups raw, peeled and chopped sweet potato

1 Tsp. Himalayan pink sea salt

1 Tbsp. organic dried oregano

¼ tsp black pepper

Create it...

Preheat oven to 375.

Make quinoa (see recipe above).

Mix flax meal for eggs (see recipe above).

Blanch kale in boiling water until it turns a bright green. Drain and roughly cut it up with ½ cup minced red onion.

Place the kale/celery, onion and sweet potato into the food processor. Add sea salt and oregano, pulse it till all is combined.

In a large bowl:

Add the cooked quinoa, the nut milk (almond), flax eggs, and the food processor veggie mixture together. Stir well until all combined.

Pour the entire mixture into a small baking pan. Approximately, a 7×12 pan. I have used my round pans too and it's cooked well in them too. Bake for 40 minutes...then enjoy!

I suggest you experiment with sizes and amounts you make. This creates a dish you can refrigerate and eat again tomorrow or freeze!

This can be an appetizer, breakfast or dinner. It can be served with a variety of other foods as it seems to go with just about everything. I like to put just a little salsa on the top of my piece before eating. Make it once and you will see what I mean!

☺ ☺ ☺

Izzy's Spicy Black Bean Tacos

Living in the southwest we love the taste of the ethnicity we are surrounded with. So many great dishes, however, most are filled with cheese. Cheese may be tasty for your palates but not so good for your hearts. Moderation is tough and consumption is high. So I am always looking for ways to enjoy the dishes I love but positively affect my heart instead of the opposite.

Gather ingredients:

Taco shells of your preference

Toppers (see below)

1 tsp extra virgin olive oil or oil of your preference

2 minced garlic cloves

1 cup red onion (chopped in small pieces)

1 – 15 oz. can of black beans, rinse and drain

½ tsp. coriander

½ tsp. paprika

1 tsp. cumin

1 tsp. chili powder

½ tsp. oregano

1 Tbsp. lime juice

¼ cup water

Salt, to taste

Create it...

Heat skillet to a medium heat and olive oil to the heated pan. Add minced garlic.

Set aside 2 Tbsp. of the raw red onions to use as a topping later. Sauté remaining onions in the skillet with the garlic. Fry lightly until it smells great and is translucent. Should not take more than a few minutes.

Add black beans, coriander, paprika, cumin, chili powder, oregano, lime juice, and water to the pan. Stir together all the of mixture.

Scoop bean mixture into your taco shell and add *toppers such as lettuce, tomatoes, avocados, etc.

George's Grilled Ratatouille Dish

This dish can be used with a wheat, white or gluten free pasta. I even recently made it with a black bean pasta that was delicious. You need to experiment on your own and remember never over cook a pasta that you are combining with veggies - so that it doesn't have a pasty taste or look to it.

Gather ingredients:

½ pound "curly" pasta (see above)

1 small eggplant - cut lengthwise into thick slices

1 small red onion - cut in half

1 med zucchini - cut lengthwise into thick slices

¼ cup olive oil, divided, plus more for grilling

1 bell pepper cut in half, stem and seeds removed

4 large tomatoes - cut crosswise into thick slices

3 to 4 tbsps. of white balsamic vinegar

¼ cup fresh parsley chopped up

Salt and pepper to taste

Create it...

Cook your choice of pasta according to package instructions. Rinse. Return to pot and set on side.

Heat your grill to medium-high and lightly oil it. Brush vegetables lightly with 2 tablespoons oil (coconut or olive), season with salt and pepper to taste. Grill all veggies turning them until they are browned and tender.

Remove vegetables from heat to a cutting board and let cool slightly. Roughly chop warm vegetables into chunks, then add into pasta. Drizzle 2 tablespoons oil and vinegar to taste. Season with salt and pepper (if needed) and parsley covered lightly on top of each bowl. Sprinkle Bragg's Nutritional Yeast on top for a little cheese flavor without the calories or fat and adds more nutrition.

This Italian flavored dish can be served with your bread of choice (sprouted, French, wheat, gluten free) and a side salad. Pasto delizioso!

☺ ☺ ☺

Shepherd's Pie with Healthy Lentils

Lentils can be a powerhouse when it comes to nutrition. This is a great substitute for other recipes like this that are higher in calories or fat. Super healthy because you are adding more veggies into your main meal!

If you like this dish and want more convenience, you can now purchase many of these veggies already diced or in florets from the grocery store and the lentils already cooked!

Preheat the oven to 400 degrees...

Gather ingredients:

2 cups of lentils cooked (see below)

1 head of cauliflower (divided into florets)

3 celery stalks - diced

3 carrots - diced

1 sm. box mushrooms (I prefer button type in this) - diced

1-2 medium onions (I prefer red) - diced

Cumin, Garlic Powder, Salt, Pepper

Drizzles of low-sodium veggie broth to use in blender.

Create it...

Prepare lentils until soft, then drain. Dice celery, carrots, ½ - 1 onion depending on your preference and mushrooms, then sauté in veggie broth until soft. Combine vegetables with lentils and the seasonings to taste. I usually omit the salt (optional) and use equal amounts of cumin, garlic power and sprinkle the pepper on top for flavor.

Then separate the head of cauliflower into florets and boil it with a half of an onion. Once they are both soft, drain well, put florets and onion in a blender, drizzle (a *very* small amount of veggie broth) and blend until soft. *The end result should have a nice thick mashed potato consistency when done.*

Take a casserole dish, fill with veggies then cover the dish with the thick blender mixture.   Bake until firm.

Serve warm. Yum. Your guest will love to spoon through the healthy white topping to get to the veggies...

"Wrap"ing it up with Sandwiches and Pita's!

Thane's Maui Sunshine Wrap

This wrap is made with fresh yellow tomatoes, giving it contrast against the other green and orange veggies. I named it after one of my favorite places on earth.

This creates 2 large wraps that you can cut in half...

Gather ingredients:

2 wraps (extra-large) I use sprouted wheat but you can use any variety.

1 yellow tomato (med), create thick slices

1 Hass avocado, peel it, slice into long thick strips, rub with a little lime and set on the side

1 sm. sweet onion (I prefer sweet Maui onions) sliced thin

4 Tbsp. lime juice (can use lemon)

1 Tbsp. Braggs Organic Apple Cider Vinegar

2 tsp maple syrup to sweeten

6 Tbsp. spicy hummus

1 cup shredded carrots

Ground black pepper

Pumpkin or sesame seeds (optional to add crunch/flavor)

Drizzles of olive or avocado oil

Create it...

Take your sliced tomato and onions and place them into a bowl. Drizzle with avocado (or olive) oil, the maple syrup, a splash of lime juice and the apple cider vinegar. FYI: Lemon juice can be used if you desire.

Warm your tortillas in the oven until they are soft, so you can bend and work with them easily. Remove and spread the spicy hummus on the entire wrap.

Add 4 slices of the avocado, a few slices of tomato, the onions and shredded carrots. Toss a pinch of pepper on top. If you have want a little more flavor, you can blend together extra maple syrup, avocado oil and lime mixture and drizzle it!

Roll up your wrap carefully and I suggest folding it in a paper towel to make it easier to then slice.

I sprinkle a few pumpkin seeds on the top or even inside, some people enjoy sesame seeds or both.

Serve these bright healthy wraps with a side of fresh mango and a few organic blue chips!

☺ ☺ ☺

Grilled Portobello Pepper Sandwich

This is a quick "throw together" if you have the veggies already pre-cooked and in the fridge to make last minute sandwiches OR you can absolutely make this sandwich from scratch - it does not take that much time at all! You can also mix and match veggies. You can use your outside grill, oven or I have an awesome little panini grill that just plugs in and I am ready to go!

Gather ingredients:

1 Portobello mushroom

1 roasted red pepper

Fresh basil leaves

Hummus, plain or red pepper (make yourself or buy)

Bread of choice (I use a thick whole grain or sprouted)

Create it...

Slice your mushrooms into a medium thickness. Cut up your red pepper lengthwise. Grill both till cooked but not limp. Lightly toast your bread. Spread a layer of hummus on each side, then place a thin layer of fresh basil leaves on each side for flavor. Add your grilled peppers, mushrooms and enjoy!!!

This recipe is simple, easy to make, and great for guests that stop by OR for a lazy afternoon meal...

☺ ☺ ☺

Gramee's Green Apple Surprise Sandwich

This is a quick summer sandwich that is loaded with flavor and super healthy. Depending on how many sandwiches your creating depends on how many apples you need!

Gather ingredients:

Sliced organic green apples (thin)

Fresh romaine leaves

Whole grain mustard

Vidalia or Sweet Maui Onions slices thinly

Bread of choice (I use a dark bread, pumpernickel or rye)

Create it...

Slice your apples and sweet onions. Take a slice of bread, put a thin layer of whole grain mustard on both sides. Add one large romaine leave and then add the apples. Simple, quick, nutritious.

Sandwiches do not need to be hard or use animal protein to fill you up. Using ingredients that you really like and have hanging around - mixed with a little mustard (there is a big variety) or hummus can create a quick, tasty and healthy meal.

Enjoy!

☺ ☺ ☺

Geo's Greek Pita

The Mediterranean people certainly knows how to combine flavor with health. Pita's are *so super simple* to create quick meals with.

Grab it, stuff it, enjoy it!

Gather ingredients:

Pita Bread (I prefer whole wheat for flavor and fiber)

Romaine or spring mix lettuce.

Cucumbers slices lengthwise and thin.

Slivered almonds

Red grapes, cleaned and sliced thin

Small chopped pieces of walnuts

Green or black olives (whichever you choose)

Greek dressing of your choice.

Create it...

You can eat your pita warm or cold. I like to warm it up slightly. Open up and put a piece of greens to the bottom or side, gently stuff it with the rest of the ingredients and then drizzle Greek dressing over the insides. Honey mustard also tastes really good.

Use your imagination, you may be able to use last night's leftovers (warm or cold) to stuff a pita for your next day's lunch. Have on hand a few different salad dressings to drizzle over the insides!

Again, grab it, stuff it, enjoy it!

☺ ☺ ☺

Roast Beet Sandwich

Beets are a MAJOR superfood and worth eating a few times per week. If you have some leftover beets (or cook them just for this dish) than this is a QUICK recipe to create.

Gather ingredients:

Sliced roasted beets

Hass avocado (can use others, but Hass has great flavor)

Sweet Mustard

Vidalia onion

Whole grain bread (or...Sprouted, Pumpernickel, Rye, Gluten Free)

Create it...

Take your roasted red beet that has been refrigerated and slice it thinly along with the avocado.

Spread a layer of sweet mustard on 2 slices of bread (you can toast or eat fresh).

Add the beets, avocado and onions.

Enjoy!!! Great sandwich to eat with blue organic chips!

☺ ☺ ☺

Ashley's BLT without the B

Everyone knows the BLT, but with recent news about the effect of processed and cured meats on our bodies, I thought I'd show my readers that you don't need the "B" in your BLT to be great tasting. The secret to the crunch and salty taste – is Beanitos, a chip made from whole black beans and rice. It's a non-GMO, complete protein, hi fiber, gluten free, no MSG or preservatives, vegan, low glycemic and absolutely no trans-fat chip! *Great to use when you need a crunch IN your sandwich...*

Gather ingredients for your tasty ALT:

4 slices of your favorite healthy bread, toasted

Mustard - either a spicy, grainy or Dijon is best

Small bag of Beanitos Chips

1 large avocado, sliced thin

Romaine lettuce

Deep red tomato (sweet with lots of flavor) sliced thin

Create it...

Spread the mustard onto the toast. Add a couple of Beanitos Chips on each side, flatten gently so they cling to the mustard. Add a layer of avocado, lettuce, sweet tomato and you're done.

Crunchy, tasty and healthy!

Cold Fresh Salads Are More Than Iceberg Lettuce!

Roger Rabbits Raw Veggie Salad

This is one of my favorite salads that I can make in a variety of ways depending on the fresh ingredients I have on hand. If there is something you don't like listed here, try it without or add something in. With this type of salad, you can't go wrong. There are so many anti-oxidants in here that your cells will be happy with each and every bite!

This particular recipe makes about 7-8 cups of salad, so depending on the portion can be a great side dish for several people.

Gather ingredients and create it...

In a large bowl combine all:

1 orange bell pepper (chopped in small bites)

1 yellow bell pepper (same as above)

1 small head of broccoli (about 2 cups) chopped small

6 radishes, sliced very thin

1 cup halved red seedless grapes

1 small sweet mango cut into little pieces (about 1 cup)

1 cucumber (seedless or remove seeds chop in small bites)

2 ½ tbsp. chopped (fresh) dill

¼ cup chopped (fresh) parsley

¼ cup sunflower seeds (raw & shelled)

Create your own fresh oil free dressing in a small bowl:

2 tbsp. red wine vinegar

1 tbsp. apple cider vinegar

Squeeze in the juice of 1 fresh lemon

1 minced garlic clove

1 tbsp. Dijon mustard

1 tbsp. pure maple syrup – drizzle over ingredients to add a little sweetness.

*Some people add a little salt and pepper to taste.

Combine both bowls and toss well. I like to create this salad at least 2 hours before serving it. After being tossed, put in fridge and every 30 minutes toss the salad. Serve cold!

Suggestion – serve with a couple slices of Naan flatbread. You can buy it at the local groceries in plain, herb and whole wheat. Toast or grill or eat right out of package! For vegans, it is an easy recipe to make without eggs or milk.

Quick & Easy Four-Bean Salad

Quick to prepare hours in advance, I love salads that taste better as they marinate. It allows me to prepare the salad ahead of time, letting all the ingredients come together. I allow the container to set in fridge at least full one day or overnight. I would not mix and serve it right away. When all these ingredients meet in the middle - it is very tasty and I know that my guests will enjoy its flavor.

This is a low sugar recipe; most others call for 3 times the amount. As a side dish, this recipe results in about 10-15 servings.

Gather ingredients:

In a bowl mix:

1 can yellow wax beans

1 can red kidney beans

2 cans green beans

1 can garbanzo beans

1 small onion finely diced (I prefer red)

¼ cup unrefined organic sugar (optional)

1 teaspoon black pepper

½ cup distilled white or apple cider vinegar

¼ cup extra virgin olive oil

Create it...

Empty the cans of beans into a colander and rinse well. Put them into a large bowl that has a tight lid on it (you will be flipping it to marinate) and add the rest of the ingredients. Keep refrigerated until serving time.

Beans are very high in anti-oxidants, so this salad will boost your immune system!

Serve cold!

☺ ☺ ☺

Thumbelina's C.A.T. Salad

C = Cucumber **A** = Avocado **T** = Tomato Salad! Great for picnic lunch. Very easy and quick, it that can be thrown together in no time at all!

Gather ingredients and create it...

Cut up vegetables and herbs in bowl:

2 Avocados

1 Zucchini

1 pound of Roma tomatoes

¼ cup Cilantro – finely chopped

1 Cucumber

½ Red Onion

After combing all of the above ingredients, mix in:

Few shakes of black pepper

¼ - ½ tsp of salt (optional and by taste).

Add 2 tbsp. of Olive or Avocado Oil (if desired)

At the end, squeeze (1) medium lemon over the salad and serve! Serve cold, 2-3 people!

This is a colorful salad that would go well in the summer with a warm OR cold soup. Pita chips with be good to line up around the edge of the plate.

☺ ☺ ☺

Roasted Butter Nut Squash & Quinoa Salad

So many people are curious about what to make with the ancient grain quinoa that has gained popularity over the past few years. This is a delicious dish that is easy and delicious and bring so much nutrition to the table. Even if you have never eaten quinoa, this is a great way to try it! Mix it with roasted butter nut squash (that has a caramelized taste when roasted) and your taste buds will than you!

Turn the oven to 400 degrees...

Creates 4-6 servings...

Gather ingredients, prepare the squash and salad:

The squash:

Start with one large 3-4 lb. squash:

Remove the seeds and cut up into ½ inch cubes. You should have around 9 cups when chopped. This amount will need 2 cookie sheets lined with parchment paper.

Spread the chopped squash onto the pans and drizzle on each pan 1 tablespoon of coconut oil over the squash. Don't over crowd either one so they have room to cook. Toss to coat. Sprinkle a small amount of sea salt over the top of the oil.

Roast until the bottoms are just starting to brown. Timing may vary, it takes between 30-50 minutes depending on your oven. After 30 minutes, take a peek, then check on every 5 min so it does not burn. Light browning especially on the bottom is good as it then has a caramelized taste which is what makes this salad taste amazing.

The salad:

1 cup uncooked quinoa (use white, red or black)

1 large avocado, remove seed and chop into same size as the cooked squash

½ cup of finely sliced spinach or kale or combo

1 tsp minced garlic

½ can of black beans, rinsed well and warmed up

Fresh lemon.

Sea salt along with fresh ground black pepper to your taste

Combine it...

Quinoa is an easy grain to cook. Every bag of quinoa comes with very simple instructions if you want to make it on your stove. I make mine in my rice cooker, one of my favorite kitchen gadgets! You literally mixed it with water and it does the rest.

For *every cup of quinoa, add 1 ¾ cup of water.* Once all the water is absorbed in the cooker, the quinoa is done. Fluff with a fork and be sure cooker is off. Season the quinoa to taste with sea salt and pepper, then stir to combine. Keep the lid on until ready to use.

Next – remove the avocado pit and chop it into small bites having it ready to mix together. When the squash is done, simply combine everything in a large bowl – put the quinoa, garlic and black beans in FIRST.

Top it with all of the hot roasted caramelized squash, and then add the chopped avocado and small amount of raw greens over the top for color and added antioxidants!

Drizzle a small amount of fresh lemon juice over it all!

Enjoy immediately. *Great protein and rich in flavor!*

☺ ☺ ☺

Jeni's Jicama Salad

Jicama is one of my favorite roots. Super healthy. Contains important minerals and vitamins. Jicama is very rich in fiber, Vitamin C, potassium, iron and calcium. I love that it has minimal fat and calories and is low in sodium. You can eat it raw or cooked. When raw, it tastes kind of like an apple or pear. Do NOT eat the skin, I peel mine with a potato peeler. When you cook jicama it will absorb all the other flavors that are cooked with it. I love to add Jicama to stir fry dishes. If you have never tried Jicama, you must.

**I also like to cut one up into French fry shapes and add them to veggie trays or eat them on their own with some hummus for the dip...delicious!

Gather ingredients:

One large jicama, around 1 ½ lbs. Peel the skin off and cut it into small pieces.

½ cucumber (finely chopped)

½ yellow pepper (small cubes)

½ red bell pepper (small cubes)

½ cup red onion (finely chopped)

½ cup of cilantro (chopped)

One sweet seedless orange with skin removed and cut into 8-10 small pieces. I like to add "Cutie" oranges if available.

1/3 cup of lime juice

Cayenne & paprika

Create it...

Put all veggies in a bowl along with the oranges. Drizzle lime juice over it all. Stir well. Then sprinkle just a pinch of paprika and cayenne on top and stir lightly to mix.

Let the bowl set in the fridge for at least 30 minutes, so all the flavors can absorb before serving.

Love a GREAT Soup or Chili...

☺ ☺ ☺

Best Black Bean Soup

This bean soup can be thrown together very quickly. It's great for those on a busy schedule or for the person who doesn't like to cook but wants a warm and tasty homemade soup (instead of canned, which for many may be their only option – till now).

I have made this soup for years and what I like is you can change up its flavor by using different salsas (really hot or mild or sweet). Try it a few different ways and you will come up with a flavor that you absolutely love.

Beans are LOADED with antioxidants, protein and other great nutrients. If you are vegan/vegetarian, then you probably already have them incorporated into your diet. If you have a gastrointestinal system that cannot handle beans very well you may want to try an enzyme to take with it (Beano) or start eating beans a little every day until your system is use to them.

Beans are a superfood in my eyes and if you can put them into your diet 3-4 times per week in some type of meal (chili, soup, on salads, etc.) your body will thank you.

Gather ingredients:

Get a small soup pot ready to go and add:

Add 2 - 15 ounce cans undrained organic black beans (I try to buy them in BPA free cans or cook in my pressure cooker and freeze them).

1 can organic vegetable broth (16 oz.)

½ cup salsa (chose your flavor and degree of hotness)

1 Tbsp. of chili powder

Create the rest...

Take *2 scallions* and cut them up, fry gently on the stove till they soften or brown lightly then add to the mixture above.

Cook soup on stove for about 15 minutes till nice and hot. Top with a little fresh chopped cilantro.

If you eat cheese products, you can also serve the soup with a lightly shredded cheese or sour cream or yogurt (optional). Vegans can add nutritional yeast or a great vegan cheese to flavor.

Robust Vegetable Couscous Soup

Couscous is a grain made of semolina and durum wheat. They use it often in traditional Mediterranean dishes. I love cooking with it because it absorbs the flavor of the liquids. You can buy this grain in any local store for your convenience.

Gather ingredients:

*10 oz. package of couscous. Go ahead and prepare by boiling 2 cups of water, add the couscous and then turn off heat and let set for about 12 – 15 minutes. Keep lid on tight and let set while you make the rest of the soup.

1 medium onion diced up (yellow preferred)

4 cups of vegetable stock

4 stalks of celery chopped into med/large chunks

4 carrots chopped into med/large chunks

2 cups of chopped butternut squash into med chunks

5 medium size peeled potatoes chopped into med chunks

15 oz. can of drained chickpeas

2 tsp of turmeric

1 tsp ground cumin

½ cup fresh dill chopped

1 tsp crushed red pepper flakes

¼ tsp salt (optional)

Create it...

In a medium soup pot sauté the onion in ½ of a cup of the vegetable stock. Cook on medium heat until you can see the onions are clear (translucent) which should take 4-6 minutes. Add the celery, carrots, butternut squash and chickpeas. Cook about 7-10 minutes till veggies are becoming soft.

Then add the potato chunks, the remainder of the veggie stock, the dill, turmeric, red pepper flakes, cumin and salt if desired. Heat to boiling and then once it does, reduce to medium heat for about 30 minutes when everything should be tender.

Place couscous in a bowl and add a serving of the soup on top.

Love eating this with a side of toasted Naan or Pita bread!

Pumpkin Black Bean Quinoa Soup

If you haven't already noticed, I believe eating well should not take all day to cook yummy recipes. Many of my recipes are healthy with added herbs and spices but contain high nutrient foods such as the pumpkin in this recipe. In about 30 minute this soup can be done and ready for your family to enjoy!

Serves 3-4 people.

Gather ingredients:

1 tablespoon olive oil

1 diced onion

1 diced red chili pepper

5 cloves of diced garlic (or use the equivalent in the jars you can buy at the store)

3 cups cubed pumpkin

1 teaspoon ground cumin

½ tsp dried oregano

½ tsp crushed red pepper flakes

½ cup quinoa (white or red)

20 oz. can black beans (rinse and drain them well)

5 cups vegetable broth (organic if possible)

2 bay leaves

Pumpkin seed, avocado & line (optional – see below)

Create it...

Heat olive oil in pan over medium heat with the onion for a few minutes then add the garlic and red chili peppers. Add pumpkin and spices, cook for a couple minutes.

Add 2 cups of the vegetable broth and the quinoa. Bring to a boil, cook for 5 min then add the remaining vegetable broth. Bring to another boil then add the beans and bay leaves. Then just simmer the soup for 5-10 minutes or longer if you have time.

Then garnish it. Your home will smell amazing!

GARNISH: I suggest sprinkling on some pumpkin seeds on top then add some avocado and a lime.

Laura's Green Is Good Broccoli Soup

If a vegetable was to get an award, broccoli would be one of the top winners for "Superfoods of the Year!"

Gather ingredients:

1 tablespoon butter (I use Vegan butter)

1 tablespoon extra-virgin olive oil

1 stalk celery, chopped

1 med. red onion, chopped

2 cloves garlic, chopped

1 teaspoon chopped fresh parsley

8 cups chopped broccoli (the stems and florets)

2 cups water

4 cups organic reduced-sodium vegetable broth

½ cup nut milk (I use unsweetened vanilla almond)

½ teaspoon salt (only if desired)

Freshly ground pepper to taste

Create it...

Heat butter and oil in a pan over medium heat until the butter melts. Add celery and onion. Cook, stirring occasionally, until both are soften, 5 - 6 minutes. Add garlic and parsley, stir lightly until you smell the fragrance in 10-15 seconds.

Stir in chopped broccoli. Add water and broth; bring to a light simmer over high heat. Reduce heat and cook until very tender, about 8 -10 minutes.

In batches, pour the soup into your blender until smooth. Stir in nut milk along with the salt (if desired) and pepper.

Great low calorie, high protein soup that is a superfood you should include into your life at least a few times per week! Serve it with a sandwich or salad or perhaps your favorite slice of a thick healthy bread!

<u>Kaileigh's Kreamy Tomato Basil Soup</u>

Another great soup filled with antioxidants and anti-aging ingredients. Can have it ready in less than 30 minutes and is delicious to compliment a dinner or make it the main dish by adding pita bread or naan bread on the side. This brings back memories of when my children were young and they loved to eat tomato soup with a grilled cheese sandwich.

This recipe creates about 3-4 servings.

Gather ingredients:

1 cup raw cashews (soak them in water for 20 min BEFORE starting recipe so they are ready)

¼ cup diced celery

1 cup diced onions

4 cloves garlic

¼ cup fresh basil

24 oz. can of tomatoes (strained)

1 ½ cup vegetable broth

¼ cup unsweetened almond milk, plain or vanilla works

2 tablespoons extra-virgin olive oil

1 bay leaf

1 Tbsp. tomato paste

½ tsp Pink salt (Himalayan)

Create it...

Have all your veggies prepared. Add the garlic, onions, celery, olive oil, bay leaf and salt to a skillet. Sauté' on medium heat until the onions become soft. Add the tomato paste and strained tomatoes along with the almond milk, vegetable broth and lightly stir until combined well. Let simmer for 15 minutes.

Then take the soup mixture and place into blender, strain the cashews (from soaking) and add them *along with fresh basil.* Blend until your favorite consistency, I like mine creamy and smooth.

Serve in bowls with a little hemp seeds on top for added protein along with fresh basil. Toast (I use sprouted wheat) matches up well with this. Delicious!

Very Easy Vegetable Chili

Easy. Healthy. Full of antioxidants!

Creates about 6-8 servings!

Gather ingredients:

1 tablespoon olive or avocado oil

¾ cup chopped carrots

1 cup chopped onions (I sometimes use green onions)

3 cloves minced garlic

1 cup green bell pepper, chopped

1 cup red bell pepper, chopped

¾ cup celery, chopped

1 tablespoon chili powder

1 ½ cups fresh mushrooms, chopped

Chop up - 1 (28 ounce) can of whole peeled tomatoes with liquid

1 (19 ounce) can kidney beans with liquid

1 (11 ounce) can Organic non-GMO whole kernel corn, undrained

1 Tbsp. ground cumin

1 ½ tsp. dried oregano

1 ½ tsp. dried basil

Create it...

Heat oil in a large saucepan over medium heat. Sauté the carrots, onions and garlic until tender. Stir in green pepper, red pepper, celery, and chili powder. Cook until vegetables are tender, about 5-6 minutes.

Stir in mushrooms, and cook another 4 minutes. Add tomatoes, kidney beans, and corn. Season with the spices then bring the pot to a boil, stir, then reduce heat to medium. Cover, and simmer for 20 minutes, stirring occasionally.

House will smell amazing, chili will be warm and healthy!

Those Darn Healthy Desserts

Amber's Apple Crisp

I recommend using *"organic"* apples as possible to lower your exposure to the chemicals that most apple farms use. No matter what, please be sure to wash apples off well with a veggie/fruit wash or vinegar/water combo. Never eat the apple seeds.

Turn the oven on 375 degrees...

Gather, prepare and create:

1 large lemon cut in half to drizzle over apple

8 cups of apples thinly sliced – I believe that crisp and tart apples work better than the sweeter varieties. I use

Granny Smiths and Empire. However, use whatever you have on hand, chances are it will be tasty no matter what!

Place apples in large bowl, squeeze the juice of one lemon over them.

In a separate bowl:

1 cup of butter (I use Earth Balance Vegan Organic Buttery Spread)

¾ cup of unbleached flour

1 ½ cups light brown sugar

1 ½ cup quick cooking oats

2 Tbsp. cinnamon

1 Tbsp. nutmeg

¼ cup water

1 cup nuts (I use ½ cup small walnut pieces and ½ cup slivered almonds)

2/3 cups raisins

Mix the flour, brown sugar, cinnamon, nutmeg and oats together, then place the butter into the dry mix and fold it in causing small to medium lumps of this wonderful topping.

Spray a glass 9 x 13 Pyrex dish lightly.

Put all 8 cups of apples into pan.

Sprinkle into mixture, 1/3 cup of raisins and pour 1/4 cup of water over apples. Then scatter the topping evenly all over the top. Place nuts and remainder of raisins on top.

Place into oven for 45 minutes.

When done, let cool briefly and eat warm by itself or over your favorite ice cream.

☺ ☺ ☺

Nick's Nut Butter Fudge Squares

The secret ingredient to these delicious squares of nut butter is coconut oil. When cooking, I use coconut oil when it's needed because of the healthy fats it contains. It boosts your immune system and helps improve and maintain other major organs.

Creates about 8 servings.

Gather ingredients:

½ cup of a nut butter (some people use peanut butter; others use almond or cashew)

2 Tbsp. soft or melted coconut oil

2 tablespoons real maple syrup

¼ tsp. real vanilla extract

¼ teaspoon salt (scant amt.)

Create it...

Combine all of your ingredients into a glass bowl. Stir well. If the fudge is too hard to mix, try microwaving the bowl for about 15 seconds, this will help soften or smooth.

Pour the fudge into a BPA free container lined with either plastic wrap or parchment paper. Place the container into the freezer and allow 35-40 minutes for the fudge to set.

After the fudge has hardened, remove the pan from the freezer and let sit for 5 minutes. Using a pretty sharp knife, cut the fudge into squares. Place the fudge into a freezer bag or BPA free plastic container and store in the freezer until ready to eat.

Chances are, this is so good, you won't have any leftover to freeze!

☺ ☺ ☺

Best Black Bean Brownies

Even if you have never tried a desert like this, it is worth doing it once. Taking a well-loved dessert and making it healthier is a challenge but this one turned out quite well and is very yummy. We all know that a large portion of people LOVE CHOCOLATE. Cacao is the plant that we get chocolate from. The % of cacao is important for the antioxidant effect. I suggest serving this delicious dessert before sharing the surprise ingredient (black bean). Most people NEVER know or cannot guess. This can be put together in 15 minutes and serves 10-12 brownies.

Preheat your oven to 350 F.

Gather ingredients:

1 – 15 oz. can of black beans (drained/rinsed very well)

½ cup of pure maple or agave syrup

2 tsp pure vanilla extract

2 tbsp. cocoa powder

½ cup quick oats

¼ tsp sea salt

¼ cup coconut oil

½ tsp baking powder

½ cup of dark chocolate chips. Can add up to 2/3 of a cup if you desire.

Create it...

In a food processor, mix all the ingredients together except chips, blending until completely smooth. Blend well. After it is really smooth, stir in chocolate chips and pour into a greased 8×8 pan. OPTIONAL: Sprinkle 1/3 cup of dark chips on top and/or 1/3 cup small pieces of walnuts.

Bake the brownies for approx. 16-18 minutes. Let them cool 10-15 minutes before trying to cut into them. After they cool, if they look undercooked at all, you can place them in the fridge for 4 hours *or* overnight. This will make the brownies firm up enough to cut and serve.

When treating your friends, serve them first, and then reveal the secret ingredient. In all the times I've served bean desserts, not one single person who didn't know beforehand has ever guessed!

Chia Pudding with Pumpkin Spice

The best part about Chia Seeds is that they are super nutritious AND easy to create recipes with. Even if you have never tried chia seeds, please do. You will be amazed how much you will like its health benefit and versatility. Chia seeds are loaded with protein, calcium, fiber and omega 3 fatty acids. They can easily be added to your daily diet. Here is a recipe I have used for years. The pumpkin pudding seems to be well loved (along with chocolate) all year around however, tastes extra special at the holidays!

For 2 servings!

Place all of these ingredients into a blender until you have a smooth consistency:

3 cups of coconut milk

2 tsp. of real vanilla extract

½ cup of 100% pumpkin puree (unflavored)

2 tbsp. pumpkin pie spice

2 tbsp. honey

Then...

Pour ½ cup of chia seeds into a large mason jar then add your liquid mixture. Close the lid securely and shake the container. After shaking, place the container in the refrigerator for at least 2-3 hours so that the chia seed absorb the all the liquids and forms a gel.

When you serve it, it tastes great with a little cinnamon powder sprinkled over it.

Enjoy...

Strawberry Chia Pudding

Chia seeds have been around for thousands of years. Some people act like it is like a new age thing – it is not. Chia seeds are versatile and among the healthiest foods on the planet. They are loaded with nutrients that benefit your body and brain which is incredibly important as we age.

This recipe can be made a day or two ahead *or* throw it together when you need a delicious snack/dessert. *Every age group loves this tasty and healthy dessert.*

It serves 4-6 depending on serving size.

Gather ingredients:

16 oz. fresh strawberries, (use only organic if possible due to pesticides) clean them good removing the stem/hull

1 ½ cups coconut milk

½ cup chia seeds

¼ cup honey (more if you like it sweeter)

2 tsp real vanilla extract or 1 vanilla bean scraped

¾ teaspoon finely grated lime zest

Create it...

In a blender, place the strawberries, coconut milk, lime zest, honey and vanilla and blend until smooth. Taste, then add more honey if desired. Place the dry chia seeds in a bowl, add the strawberry mixture into it and whisk thoroughly. Let stand for 10 minutes and then whisk again.

Once done, cover well and refrigerate for at least 4 hours and up to 3 days without spoiling.

Stir it before serving. As it sits, the pudding may thicken. If it does, whisk in a little coconut water if you have it or just plain water.

Serve in cups or bowls and you can garnish with strawberries, coconut flakes or slivered almonds. Nutrient strong for all ages! Kids love eating AND making this dessert!

Snacks ...Toppings... And More!

☺ ☺ ☺

Beans & Avocado Toast

This is a favorite of mine mainly because of the taste and that it is full of protein and very filling. This is a great snack or breakfast and goes over well with kids who enjoy eating Mexican dishes.

Gather ingredients:

1-2 slices of the bread of your choice -> I prefer Ezekiel Sprouted Bread, but you can use a variety. Gluten free, whole wheat, etc.

Ripe Avocado

1 can of vegetarian refried beans (no lard in it)

White onion

Prepare it...

Slice up avocado. Slice up onion into thin strips. Open can of beans and if too thick can add a little bit of water.

Toast bread. Cover it with a layer of beans. Take multiple thin slices of avocado to cover the beans. Add a few strings of Jicama. Enjoy!

You could put a thin layer of salsa over the top of the avocado to have a little spicier flavor to your toast!

☺ ☺ ☺

Cashew Sour Cream

I actually found this recipe a couple years ago and love it. Not sure who to give credit to as many cooks use this recipe in place of sour cream and it can be used on a variety of dishes especially Mexican ones. I love it because when my friends or family come over, they are all able to eat it. It is milk free, gluten free, grain free, sugar and soy free and of course vegan. You may need to get use to its different taste than a milk based sour cream, but trust me when you do you will love it's taste and tremendous health benefits.

When you use cashews for this dish, soaking them overnight is part of the process. How easy can that be?

Gather ingredients:

1 ½ cups of raw cashews, soaked (see below)

¾ cup purified water

2 tsp. apple cider vinegar

2 Tbsp. fresh lemon juice

½ tsp. fine sea salt (I use pink Himalayan)

Prepare it...

Place the raw cashews in a bowl, cover with water and put on cabinet for the night. Soak them for 8 hrs. If you need to make some quickly, you can pour "boiling water" directly over the cashews and soak them for about 1 hour. When they are done, rinse and drain well.

Either way, place the drained cashews in your blender. Add the water, vinegar, lemon and salt. Set on high until mixture is super smooth. If it becomes too thick add just a little water to thin it. When it's done, place into a non

BPA air-tight container and put into refrigerator. Your cashew cream will thicken and be ready to use in a couple hours.

FYI: You can also freeze the cream up to one month for any immediate needs. I have BPA free ice cube trays and muffin tins that I freeze them in. Once frozen, I pop them out and put them into freezer bags. Easy and tasty!!!

☺ ☺ ☺

Max's Mango Pineapple Salsa

This is one of those salsas that you can use for an appetizer, to add flavor to a dish or as a salad topper. Because we travel to the islands often, my taste buds for mangos' and pineapples' is very strong, without a doubt! Heck, I like to squeeze mangos over my green salads instead of using a processed salad dressing. Plus, both of these delicious fruits can be grilled and added to sandwiches and more!

Gather ingredients:

1 red bell pepper

1 mango

2 cups pineapple

1 cup sweet cherry tomatoes

¼ cup red onion

¼ cup cilantro

2 Tbsp. freshly squeezed lime juice

Just a pinch of red chili powder & cayenne pepper (optional for a little heat) Salt and pepper to taste only.

Chop the mango, pineapples and red bell pepper into small cubes. Cut the sweet cherry tomatoes in half. Mince the red onion and then finely chop the fresh cilantro.

Mix all of the above ingredients together in a large bowl, squeezing in the lime juice. For a little heat, add a pinch of the cayenne pepper and chili powder along with salt and pepper to taste. Mix together all really well.

Let set aside to allow the juices combine together in the refrigerator then serve with anything you want.

Very versatile and yummy salsa!

☺ ☺ ☺

Kiel's Koconut Baked Avocado Fries

Americans loves avocados, actually the world loves avocados! Plain, in salsa, added to dishes, mashed, whole, in slices – wherever and whenever! Avocados offer a huge health benefit especially for the aging population. It's great for our skin, eyes, brain and just about every cell. Even though it is a fat, it's categorized as a "good fat" and has tremendous health benefits. I am always looking for ways to prepare avocados as an appetizer for when my family and friends come over. The usual is a Mango-Avocado Salad (see recipe in this book). So when I came across the idea to make a coconut fry – I was so excited. This recipe is easy and can be made in very little time.

This recipe will give you 2-3 servings if you just want a few pieces each. I usually prepare more as they are a real hit! If that's your situation, then just double or triple the recipe to start with.

I use a non-stick baking sheet. Depending on the serving, this one currently is for 3 people.

Heat oven to 400 degrees.

You will need 3 bowls for this short process.

Gather ingredients:

Start with Bowl 1:

½ tbsp. of flaxseed mixed with 1 ½ tbsp. of water. Combine and put into fridge.

Then take:

One large avocado. Cut it in half, then cut each half in 3-4 slices. Set aside.

In a 2nd medium bowl combine:

½ tsp smoked paprika

¼ tsp black pepper

½ tsp onion powder

3 T arrowroot powder

1 tsp garlic powder

In the 3rd bowl put your:

¾ cup of unsweetened coconut

Now take out the bowl of flaxseed mixture from your fridge.

Create it...

Simple → Take one piece of avocado with a fork and drag it thru the spice/arrowroot mixture covering it completely. Then dip that piece into the flaxseed mixture covering as much as you can. Finally, dip the piece into the coconut bowl and then place onto pan.

It's that easy!

Bake at 400 degrees for 5-8 minutes or till the edges of the coconut brown start to brown. These tasty fries can be served alone or with a salsa type tomato dip.

You will really enjoy this "green fry" as the start to your meal, party or cookout!

Esther's Roasted Wings Cauliflower Style

This is a simple snack that could be a big hit at a football game or party. It literally can replace the taste of chicken wings with its spicy bite of flavor. Make them once, you will see what I mean.

Serves 5-6 guests...

Preheat oven to 400F.

Gather ingredients:

1 head cauliflower (you can cut or buy already cut up)

½ tsp. ground cumin

½ tsp. smoked paprika

1 tsp. mild chili powder

½ tsp. garlic powder

¼ tsp. chipotle chili powder (optional but gives it a bite!)

½ tsp. salt (to taste or optional)

Create it...

Line a large baking sheet with parchment paper to prevent sticking.

Cut or purchase the cauliflower in bite-sized florets. Keep them the same size if possible. Rinse with clean water and shake them off but don't dry. Then spread the florets out on the baking sheet.

Combine all of the seasonings in a bowl. Sprinkle over each floret, turning each one so that all sides are seasoned. Sometimes I put the seasonings in a gallon plastic bag and drop the florets in, fluffing them around. It may coat some more heavily, however, see what works for you.

Bake in preheated oven for 15 minutes. Turn florets over and bake another 15 minutes. They are done when they are beginning to brown in spots. Remove and serve warm with your favorite dipping sauce.

There is nothing like a spicy appetizer on a weekend afternoon or a football Sunday... enjoy!

Pesto with Heart Healthy Hemp

I have learned to love hemp seed over the past couple of years. Hemp has a nutty flavor, is a great source of plant based protein, helps with menopause, aids in digestion and reduces your risk of heart disease. It is super nutritious if you have never tried it, I highly suggest that you do. Recipes are popping up all over with this seed, so I am sure you will find something for you.

Makes 2 cups

Gather ingredients:

2 small cloves garlic

¾ cup organic hemp seeds

5 cups organic packed greens (I used spring mix, others use spinach) Use any leafy greens or herbs that you like.

Juice of 1 lemon

¼ cup olive, avocado or coconut oil

¼ cup grated Parmesan cheese (or use ½ cup nutritional yeast or a nondairy dried cheese)

¾ tsp salt

¼ tsp pepper

2 - 4 Tbsp. water pending consistency

Create it...

Place garlic cloves in a food processor and pulse a few times to finely chop, then add hemp seeds with half the greens and whirl until greens are mostly chopped.

Scrape down the sides, add remaining greens and blend again. When all the greens are mostly chopped, add remaining ingredients and blend until smooth. You can keep adding water to achieve a sauce-like consistency.

Taste for seasonings and add more salt, pepper or lemon as needed.

This is a great recipe that creates a pesto you can put on sandwiches, add to hot pasta or to pizza. Super creamy and tasty!

The Edible Fountain of Youth
EAT THE WAY YOU WANT TO LOOK

485991R00042

Made in the USA
Middletown, DE
11 January 2018